THE FIRST FIFTY POEMS

●

Jenefer Ann Murray

Published by Palores Publications 2008

The First Fifty Poems
Copyright © Jenefer Ann Murray 2008

Front Cover:
Copyright © Jenefer Ann Murray 2008

ISBN 978-0-9556682-3-4

Published by:
Palores Publications,
11a Penryn Street,
Redruth,
Cornwall.
TR15 2SP

Designed and printed by:
ImageSet,
63 Tehidy Road,
Camborne,
Cornwall.
TR10 8LJ

Typeset in:
Helvetica 11pt
Helvetica 14pt

Foreword

As a child, although I had a ready ear for A.A. Milne, Edward Lear and Walter da la Mare, my appreciation for other poetic works tended to be impeded by a stubborn sense of logic.

"Why is the tiger burning?" I asked my governess crossly, "has somebody set fire to it?"

Later on at school I was dragged year by year through Shakespeare comma by comma and Milton, whose poems seemed remarkably irrelevant to my way of life.

Now, aged 84, I see myself as a newcomer to the miraculous world of poetry and feel as if the entire English language has been dumped on my lap — a present of unsurpassable magnificence.

Contents

The Rose	1
Bad Little Girl	2
In a Nutshell	6
Apple Trees	7
School Prefects	10
Music Story	12
Wartime Revels	16
The Arrival	17
The Trap	18
In Galway	21
Dark Night	24
The Fountain	26
London Weekend	27
The Cats of London	28
And Yet, dear Friend	29
To a Dear Friend	30
Workshop in the Solar	31
To a Poet (Noel Welch)	33
Zonal Pelargoniums	34
In Memory of Richard Dadd	35
The Lifeboat House Art Gallery	36
And There's This	38
Looking Like This	39
Brain Strangle	40
Merry Widow's Song	41
Do I Love You?	42
The Figurehead	43
Reading Poetry in Middle of Night	44
Poem Before Breakfast	46
Poem During Breakfast	47
Poem After Breakfast	48
Blissfully O.T.T. In One's Eighties	49
O.T.T. Again	50
Perhaps	51
What Has Happened?	54
The Handsome Irish Gardener	56
The Heart	58

Sad Song - Glad Song	59
Luncheon Guest	61
Henman on Court	62
The Seagull Scene	68
An Arboreal Triumph	69
Taking a Walk	71
A Strange Remark	72
Medical Students	73
Being Ill	75
Discovery	76
The Bus Load	77
Why Both?	79
The Dream	81

The Rose

This Rose
I can't believe it
what a beauty
hallo Rose
I can't remember your name
but I don't remember anybody's name
these days
so please forgive me

But you do know my name
and call me by it
I am Rose
I am your Rose
You grew me in your garden
and fed me in the Springtime
when I was hungry
you gave me water
when the skies were dry
now I am your Rose
pick me if you wish
I am here for you
that is my purpose

Bad Little Girl
a disastrous outing

She was with this old aunt
a great-aunt really, grandfather's sister
very old
seemed covered in mould
more or less
silly old great-aunt has offered
to take her to dancing class
mother, not well, says yes.
Oh dear.
"You will be good, darling, please,
as good as gold."
"Will I?" she wonders with unease
she wonders if she will
but poor mother does look ill
oh dear. Oh well....

Child holds small case in hand
something ancient found in attic
suitcase holding dancing dress
apricot colour, great success
shiny slippers, clean white socks
little posy, cardboard box
(not real flowers, wouldn't last
silk or something, sometimes feathers)
brush and comb for dark fringed hair
shiny, like shoes
needles and cotton, safety pins
extra knickers, just in case
yes, do mean in this suitcase
(have a giggle, joke is funny)
handkerchiefs for nose, if runny
things for cleaning hands and face
nothing messy, not a trace
not a speck — exactly right
except old great-aunt, crabby, shabby
all her clothes so blackly drabby
oh dear.

Have to go by bus
not in father's great dark red
thundering long-nosed Bentley
held together by leather strap

Bus too crowded, horribly hot
"Little girl will sit on my knee,"
says aunt. How dreary
"No, I'll stand, I'll be all right."
"If you stand you will be weary
before your class
now come, sit on my knee
"She's my little angel." tells all around
she often says this
they titter, politely.

aunt is hot and bony thin
child clutched fiercely
to torrid frontal fortifications
discomfort, though, has limitations
"Oh please auntie, not so tight."
"Bus is bumpy, don't be pert, miss
if you fall you might be hurt"
aunt gives child unwanted kiss
she has white whiskers
ten thousand wrinkles
some extra crinkles
clothes a bit musty, fusty and hot
everything you'd rather not.
Oh... dear....

Journey ends at last
Royal Hotel Plymouth before the blast
before that cruelty
gorgeous ballroom — chandeliers

glowing crimson, gleaming gold
white and cream and beautiful
(must try to be dutiful)
scramble into dancing rig
old aunt hopeless, clumsy, slow
how to cope she doesn't know

after, dressed in usual gear
almost very last to go
tired and hungry after class
"Now we'll go and have some tea
Goodbody's restaurant nice and near."
"Oh no, auntie, please not there."
"Nothing wrong with it, just round here."
Oh dear... oh well...

Daunting triad middle-aged ladies
piano, violin, cello
droopy toad green dresses — dull
Joyce Grenfell might have known them
slightly
lunch-time, tea-time, not twice nightly
dismal music, hard to bear
sit at table, take a cake
"Thank you."
Aunt is chatting, grown-up questions
"Did you enjoy your dancing class?"
"Um."
"Which part of it did you like best?"
mumble. "All of it. Thank you."
"Finish cake now, must catch bus."
Child disbelieving, shattered
"Oh no, auntie, always two,
must have two cakes, always do
"Not today because of bus
now be good, don't make a fuss."
Oh dear!

Patience gone and temper lost
expectations over-bossed
leaps to feet, lifts treasured case
shouting, shaking, scarlet face
"If can't have another cake
I shall throw this on the floor
where I dare say it will break"
"Don't be silly, you wouldn't dare."

Oh yes she would dare
Oh yes she would....

and flings the case with fearful force
it lands at awful auntie's feet
and there explodes, it would of course
precious contents everywhere
crushed and crumpled, mingled mangled
under table, far and wide
Outrage!
"Mercy, is the child crazed?
Don't know what's come over her,"
gasps the aunt, aghast, amazed.

Child furious, silent, glaring
everybody staring, staring
(Don't care, I don't care
and I did dare
of course I did, I knew I would
just couldn't go on being good)
waitress dash to do her best
rapid damage limitation
auntie's useless explanation
apologies and fulmination

Rush for bus, silently
not the lap again
"I will stand, I'll be all right."
old auntie swiftly falls asleep
poor old thing, a worn out heap

momentary passing pang
hope she won't begin to snore
Oh dear

Home at last, great consternation
Auntie old, remote and haughty
all mixed up with tired and brave
and bad little girl who can't behave
bad little girl who's been so naughty
No excuses, say you're sorry
So ungrateful, so unkind.
Finally, capitulation,
early brainwash, seems to me
"I was naughty, sorry, sorry."
Family overflow with blame
Sorry, sorry, full of shame
Mother with a shake of head
"Supper now and off to bed
I'll come up and see you soon."

"You did behave most awfully badly,"
says mother later, sadly, sadly
"Is old auntie going home soon?"
"Yes tomorrow not till late."
All three of them can hardly wait.

In a Nutshell

My two grandmothers
Did not like each other
One was church
One was chapel
A huge gap
Religious trap
When they met
Could see them bristle
Air full of thistle
If we'd also had the Pope
We'd all have had
To give up hope.

Apple Trees

In my grandmother's garden
There were apple trees
All about, all sorts.
Day by day
They went their way
And came to occupy our thoughts
When we were children

Observing this my grandmother said
I give you the apple trees
My dears
From now on they are yours
But I do have fears
Some of those trees are tall
There must be no fall
No tears.
Oh Granny, oh no Granny
Thank you Granny oh.
No breaking leg or arm
No harm
Is that understood?
You will be good?
Oh yes Granny, yes Granny
Thank you Granny yes.
We knew if we did not obey
They would be taken away.

She was a cantankerous old lady
And loved us.
More than we loved her
Our grandfather had not made her happy
When he was alive
And he made her sad still
Now that he was dead
But the apple trees were ours.

Don't you go breaking they branches
The gardener said, passing under.
But they're ours, Hawken
The apple trees are ours
Granny gave them to us.
He growled. Just don't pick the flowers
Gardeners are like that
You hurt what grows
You hurt them
Unless it's a weed, planning to seed
But there weren't many of them
Hawken was a good gardener
And we loved the trees
Knew no flowers no fruit
No precious loot.
Many were old, easy to hold
Some thickly branched
Painful to penetrate
Some we never climbed at all
Trunks too tall.
It was a shame Granny never came
We invited her
Come some time, see us climb.
It was my grandfather's garden really
She said he loved it
More than he loved her
But if you marry
A gardening man
You must let him go free
As much as you can
That I could easily see
When I was only three
We climbed with care
Not without an occasional dare
Collected windfalls and the rest
Lined them up
From small to best
Chose

Day by day
From the tidy rows
Handed some round in various guises
Gifts, rewards, prizes

Thank you cross old lady
Sad old lady
We owned the apple trees

School Prefects

Hefty great girls, some beautiful
Tough as half-cooked rind
Towering tall, crusted with authority
And full of savage words —
Disgusting, lazy, slack, disloyal.
Disloyal to what? The hockey team?
Let it lose or let it win
By all means let it win
I will not linger in that desert.
Lazy? I am reading.
That is not permitted in this school?
Disgusting. That double-edged description
Hangs in the air and you who speak
Are not, I think, unscathed.
Slack? No! Too tightly strung.
Jerked by prison ropes
I must appear dancing
To this discordant music
And now look, after forty years
Still I rage

Then to my amazement it was my turn
The mantle fell on me
All were not considered for that state
And I had thought to duck its leaden weight
Escape, of course, was not curriculumed.
"School Music Prefect?
No you can't refuse
An honour for your house." they said,
Awestruck tinge apparent.
Honour? Outrageous designation
Dull responsibility called joy.
For me no bugles blared
Or banners flew.
Lord, what a petty pinnacle
What trivial attainment.
More time spent in shaded chapel

(Toad green cloth, yallery glass
Even the flowers made ugly)
Handcuffed to minor music
Small organ, featureless
Uniform as ourselves
A hundred humdrum dronings
Dreary as the day
A dearth of diapasons, no drama here
Whispered dialogues — cockroach rustle —
With organ-playing teacher-woman
Relentless unfavoured drudge
Fangs incorrectly angled, awful hat
Transforming gold to mud
As many do, poor captive souls —
And everyone so serious, I laughed
And now look, after forty years
I'm laughing still
And still I rage, still I rage.

Music Story - explanatory notes

At the end of the summer term, 1940, when I was nearly seventeen, I left my rather unmusical boarding school (the headmistress was tone deaf) having taken all the Royal Academy of Music exams except the so-called Final. I was to have taken it that term but fell off my bicycle on the way back from an afternoon spent removing charlock from a field otherwise engaged — patriotic wartime occupation. I hurt an arm and couldn't practise so the exam was postponed until autumn when an examiner arrived in Plymouth.

That over, I found my father possessed by the notion that I should now have a go at the L.R.A.M. examination. I could take it next summer, he thought. My mentor was to be the wife of one of his head clerks, a small, stout, frizzle-haired primary school teacher who had recently won a local contest in Torquay for playing a piano version of Finlandia.

Having been sent to call on her I found her quite calm and eager about the enterprise. I asked whether she would play her recent triumph and she sat down briskly at her indifferent piano and stormed off at great speed, producing a stunning effect of intemperate uglification, right foot employed with wanton excess.

I returned to my mother, brought up to play the organ in church, join in the bell-ringing and disport herself at musical evenings, with a condemnatory report. "She's absolutely awful, Ma." To my surprise my mother fell into a distress.

"Oh, darling," she said, "I don't think you can refuse. Your poor father is so set on the idea and it's all arranged. To cancel it now would cause frightful difficulties. You must see. And your father is having such a hard time just now." And so he was; his partner had gone off to war, he was the Captain Mainwaring of the Local Home Guard and his only son was a Dartmouth cadet shortly to be despatched to the high seas. "If you can't do this," my mother added, "I just don't know what I shall do." The problem was indeed easy to understand.

So the primary school teacher sent off for particulars and we embarked on the project. Any idea of the usual three years training for the exam did not filter through to us. Someone along the way might have said, "For this you should practise five hours a day," but if they had I should have looked at them blankly. The ridiculous aspect of the whole thing led me to take a minimum of interest because what I wanted was to be old enough to join the WRNS which, in the long run, was what I did. And now the poem.

Music Story

I entered the doors of that musical place
And the blindfold fled from my eyes
Confusion left my listening ears
And I instantly lost my disguise
From behind closed doors did the music sound
All-pervading and all around
Fiddles, pianos, the call of the flute
A life-giving quality hard to refute
Scales and arpeggios, arcane decorations
Appoggiaturas, insane revelations
Such snatches and catches, such skilled modulations
The space was alive with incessant gradations
And I, all alone, at the foot of the wall
What a cliff, what a mountain impossibly tall
I so lowly among the elite
A fool with shocked reluctant feet
For I had arrived by an ignorant path
Despatched from a totally different hearth
Admired by people who did not know
The heaven above or the abyss below
I knew it well but could not understand
(as I thumped and cavorted, displayed with the band)
Why they clapped and applauded and piled me with praise
Said I was wonderful, language ablaze
With ridiculous nonsense, a flowering weed
That crassly disseminates dangerous seed.
I did have some talent, I still have it now
I still play in public and still take a bow
But performance was faulty then, skills incomplete
I didn't like work and was tempted to cheat
If confronted with something a little too tough
I'd neglect the precision and leave it quite rough
I would camouflage round it and nobody saw
So I'd do it again and I'd do it some more.
But where was the dignity, where was the joy?
I was employing a false alloy
No alloy of silver, an alloy of dust

No alloy of gold but an alloy of rust
And I never could play in the least as I wished
So when they said, "Good," I was thoroughly dished.
I passed the exams though with moderate marks
I took them for interest, I took them for larks
They didn't seem serious, work I did not
For I knew what I was and I wasn't a swot
And here I was now in this elegant place
Unfinished, unpolished, with egg on my face.
When it came to my turn and was time to go in
I knew that my presence was absolute sin
They asked me some questions, I got them all wrong
My brain had gone missing and didn't belong
I knew without thought that my best was their worst
It took more than I'd got to banish their thirst
For the excellent delicate cascades of notes
So abundantly furnished with classical quotes
Which of course they expected and usually had
But now they had me, so unusually bad.
I left that place with a soul like a tip
With my thoughts upside down and a trembling lip
My smiling companions said, "How did it go?"
I couldn't reply but they soon seemed to know
They soon seemed to tell that it hadn't gone well
Though they couldn't imagine the absolute hell.
We turned to the left and we started to walk
I tried not to cry but I still couldn't talk
Some workmen were digging, the war had begun
And all sorts of digging was still to be done
I threw all my music straight into a drain
Croaking,"I'll never play the piano again."
My brother retrieved it, the workmen were dumb
The rest of the world unaccountably numb
For weeks I was silenced and longed to be dying
The horrible truth was I hadn't been trying
I couldn't stand music, not even a note
As if I were drowning without any boat
I'd go into the garden and think other thoughts
My head all confounded with crosses and noughts

Oh hell and damnation, oh what a mistake
In the end I'd re-muster and do a retake
I'd play Warsaw Concerto in African climes
Provide a sound backdrop for concerts and mimes
I'd round up the boogie, so basic, such fun
When I first played it well then I knew I had won
But before I did that there was work to be done.
I'm really not brilliant, I'll play if invited
And if you enjoy I'll be truly delighted
I've oceans of music stacked up on a shelf
I'll get some of it down and I'll play for myself
If anyone says, "Shall we try some duets?"
I will instantly cry, "Oh how lovely, do let's."
So go practise your music each day of the year
And please do your best or you'll suffer, my dear.

Wartime Revels

An azure dress she wore, lent by a godmother,
With skirts that flew and floated as she danced
And scarlet beads owned by her mother many years,
Now offered with amusement.
Her hair was somewhat curled and pinned — a work,
A worry, flowered for occasions like that night
The room — large, windows curtained black
No royal midnight blue permitted,
No shining moon allowed, no dawn let in.
And in that festive space, music - swung and whirling,
Light-spun and lustred with glass and hoarded wine,
He stood, polished, older, from a foreign land
Forced to leave and stretched with grief.
"My dear," he said, laughing, "How you do enjoy yourself."
Sorrow clear in the lined and handsome face
But for that moment less, a little dimmed.
But she, aged seventeen and driven by the dance
Could not pause for pity.

Eugene Priszchietsky at RAF Newton, Polish training aerodrome. When his course ended, he was posted to RAF Syerston, a bomber station just down the road. Shortly afterwards, he was killed. He did not die unwept.

The Arrival

He stepped off the train
Wearing a leather coat
And a purple hat, wide-brimmed,
Which clutched at my heart.
"Oh, I adore your hat."
I cried, clasping him.
"I knew you'd like it."
He said, eyes gleaming.
We rushed home.

The Trap

I did not want that child
Not then
Life turned dull
No smoking no drinking
No dancing no fun
Nowhere to run
Escape outlawed.

I saw myself ugly
Each week more misshapen
Cherished clothes neglected
Images rejected
Smocks were current then
Shocks in looking glass
A dreary fashion.

I should be radiant
Joy, anticipation
Gentle maternal expression
I, aware only
Of repression
Of depression. No
Not like that.

Waiting was a malady
Birth not decent
I had not known
Such matters.
And now this savage!
Crying so, a tyrant
All the dragging hours

Infant essentials
Unexpected
Efforts to help
Misdirected
Necessities not understood
Problems arrived
Uncontrived

I tried and tried
Attempted, strived
To travel to unravel
This unheralded
Uncontrolled ongoing
Repetitive
Nightmare

Her father - young
Conventional
Ignorant as I
Distanced himself
Babies not his concern
And he had work to do
And meant to do it

Harsh Africa frowned.
Her infant strength
Drowned, insufficient
Death unconsidered
Unsuspected
One night she died
A life of small length

Now we were strangled
Choked in different maze
We cried, we wept
Lived unbalanced
Unshielded desert
Unknown sands
Shifted under foot.

Thoughts bruised
As if by blows
As if by thrown stones
All that was hers
Sword sweeps
Dodged, denied
Eventually thrust away

It was a trap
And we
And she
Trapped

In Galway

Mounting the stairs in this Irish hotel
Carry cot with baby in one hand
Suitcase in the other
Full of things for babe in cot
This and that, what not
Tons of stuff, hope enough
Handbag, long strap, slung round neck
Hint of fast approaching wreck
Glasses dark for outside sun
Travelling from South to North
Back and forth
Just arriving, miles of driving —
When I met a short, thick man
Bounding down
Two or three steps at a leap
Sure he'll end up in a heap
Tightened grip on carry cot
Because one never knows quite what
Might come to pass upon the stair
Of any hotel, anywhere.
Perhaps encounter jovial soul
Likely to have had a jar
Or two too many in the bar.

"Have ye got a son'?"
He asked me, stopping.
"No, it's a daughter actually."
Oh to get to our room
Baby must be simply sopping
"No, I mean have ye got a son'?"
Last word rhymes with sit upon
"Er, no, a daughter, little girl."
I told him kindly. Brain
As thick as body, it would seem.
His face twisted, disbelief, derision,
"No, no, I mean have ye got a son'
A SON'?
You look as though you might."

Temporary indecision
Obliteration, dislocation
"He means a song." said husband helpfully
Coming up behind
"Have I got a song?
What on earth does he mean?"
Small developing scene.
Did he mean, in the luggage?
Sheet music crumpled into baggage?
"I think he wants you to sing."
Husband said gravely: he had Irish blood.
"Sing? What now?" I was weary
One often is, when with a baby
I looked at the short, thick man
He looked at me
We were baffled, all three.
"We're having a party," he explained
"Oh.... well, as you see
we've only just arrived and —"
"Not now, not now, ma'am,
this evening.
We want a turn from every guest
There'll be prizes for the best
So, HAVE ye got a son'?"
"Oh well, no, I'm afraid I haven't."
babble, babble
overstrained goosey gabble
"I do play the piano but I'm afraid
I'm rather out of practice, what with
One thing and another ...."
(in fact since I'd become a mother)
"My wife is tired,"
husband interposed
thoroughly enjoying it all
I supposed
People listening in hall
I perceived

"We must go and unpack
We'll see you later." Charming smile
to short, thick , baffled chappie
A bit disturbed, a bit unhappy
Poised so eager on the stair
Disappointed in his quest,
a strangely disobliging guest
"Carry on darling," husband said
"No more of this, a rest instead."

"Oh dear, do you think that we
irrespective of the hour
Could have some tea
Sent up for you and me?
A.S.A.P.?

Dark Night

I had a house once
For nearly thirty years
If the moon was missing
The sky clouded
House lights out
Curtains drawn back
Darkness was there and to spare
Nothing to be seen
Only black.

Sounds more acute
Outside restive
Murmur of trees
Leaves turn in breeze
Distant train passes
Beyond the hill
A stretch of fields
Windblown grasses
Fox bark, instant alarm
Presence of infinite harm
Multiple murder
Becomes a must
Frantic blood lust.

Owl shriek, voice of bat
Tell the truth
I can't hear that
I could when young
And remember it now
As a hoarse squeak
Uncouth
When I could hear it
My parents could not
Now my children can
A sound for youth.

Inside more festive
Gorgeous dark
Flower scent through window
Ancient house, creak of wood
Rustle of sheet, whisper in ear
"Shall we, my darling, my dear?"
"But I cannot see
You might be anyone."
Imagination free.
A laugh, "So I might
Stranger in the Night"

But of course it is he
I feel his thin gold necklace
Fall on my skin
I gave it to him
A whim
"I think I should like
A bejewelled man."
One should be exotic if one can
And he loves the chain
Sometimes loves me
Sometimes not

All's well for the moment
Black black night
Nothing to see
Just all the rest
And for a time
Just being will do
Me and you

The Fountain
(Dartington Hall Gardens)

This garden
inhabited by children
just a few
adventurous ones
escaping the mandates
hiding in bushes
racing between trees
in the shadows
observing the swans
against the rules.

Two swans entwined
graceful, unmoving
no feathers here
stone, rough to the hand
forms a path for rising water
in the garden among the flowers
shades and spaces
a single jet up and up
falling gently
now and then

London Weekend

Sunday morning
world gone quiet
hum of plane behind the cloud
shaft of sunlight, yellow flower
and a bird, singing.

The Cats of London

The cats of London are wild and free
They roam the city for all to see
Sit by the window, watch them go by
With cautious tread and crafty eye.

The cats of London are lean and quick
They're up to the mark and they don't miss a trick
A threat to each other to birds and to mice
They're elegant, beautiful, not very nice
Here for a moment, gone in a trice.

The cats of London are hunters skilled
A clamouring stomach has got to be filled
Slinking and slouching, cruel to excess
A leap and a crunch, one sparrow the less.

The cats of London are fighters keen
Treasured and cared-for or scruffy and mean
They gather on rooftops and howl in the night
A hissing and scratching reverse of polite
Do let's get on with it, bother the height.
We shall not fall off in a tumbling arc
Because as you know we can see in the dark.

The cats of London are sleek and fat
Spoiled and pampered and sat on a mat
On a chair, on a throne with salmon and sole
And fiddlers three like Old King Cole.

The cats of London are groomed for shows
With coiffeured hair and pedicured toes
Look this way and smile if you please
A disciplined life but a life of ease.

And Yet - dear Friend....

Old ailing heap, aflame with courage
Half-aided in half-alien world,
Prisoner of harsh-taught courtesies
And so, constrained even among friends
To banish silence. She blunders on —
Stories twenty times told, facts askew.
Words like a torrent of dry stones
Or bells in a glaring sun
Fall like hammers on the undefended mind.

And yet — dear friend ....

To A Dear Friend

You cast a starry glaze
Over my days,
A thousand insights into my nights
As I lie, awake and happy
In my house by the sea.
Where have you been, you
Over the decades never met?
And now, with another.
I do not mind, you are
In my head, in my brain
Handsome and all the rest.

Your old arm, sleeve rolled up
Lies on the table as you speak.
I would like — but no....
That way, we do not go.
Remember, please, to stay content.
Nothing further can be meant,
Old as we are, beyond
The cares and tatters of the heart,
Those risks and sins not now a part
Of this new sea in which I fall
Unafraid, not drowned, amazed
Treading the fringes of your world.

Oh my dear friend
You cast a starry glaze
Over my ending days.

Workshop in the Solar

There they sit, each in her own state
Frontiers undefined, free trade
Here the mind may be refurbished
Like a palace.

Voices fill the room, a hum
Light from many angles falls
On samples fixed around the walls
On tables strewn with fabric
Silks and cottons, organza, scrim
Hessian, canvas, calico
Such names, such words
Steps along the journey
Of a thousand miles or more

Light fills the air with firework flash
Of jewelled threads, piled and heaped
Turns gold to a gilded dazzle
Pinpoints a figured fragment.
Books travel round, hand to hand
Beacons, signposts of work
From other times, other styles
Other people.
A tutor, decorative as may be
Circulates slowly
Sparking with ideas, sparing with answers
Find your own if you can

Designs follow their winding ways
To dwindle or develop as they may
Dangerous, delicate, daft, dull
Or elegant — eagle flight to the mark
Shapes and shadows, leaves to fill a forest
Cascades of flowers, free forms balanced
Windowed spaces, sun-shafted skies
Patterns, borders, strips and stripes
Chequered, latticed, random —

The path is not direct and some are lost
Bedizened not caparisoned their flighty horses prance
Fretted by failure, spurred by sudden chance
Beset by doubt, encouraged by each other
Thoughts racing to hold the darting dragonfly
On with the dance, on with the dance

I knew that there were many mansions
I saw them white, on a hill
With birds and gardens, very far away
Now that unmeasured distance seems illusion
I walk among those mansions
Look back the other way across the miles
To lower lands I usually tread.

To A Poet
for Noel Welch

You were always special
Slightly haloed
Alone now but full of light.
Delicate you are
A fierce and gentle lady
Sword in hand,
Skilful with your wishes.

Such a very fine mind
Wreathes around your world
Keeps it rare and beautiful
And you beautiful in it.
Butterflies, cage-birds free to fly
Music, sunlight, wind-stir
Lilies and irises, blessings,
A million bluebells —
Infinity always present.

Zonal Pelargoniums

Resplendent pomp
Unequivocal visual romp
New development today
A threat
Greenfly aggression
Greenflies make green fingers
Manipulative repression
Retrogressive progression
If I didn't stop you
The plants would
Those leaves don't do you
Any good

A rash attack
Pelargoniums fight back
Bold and blissful exhibitionists
Greenfly abolitionists
These trouble-makers
Emerald crooks
Increase like locusts
Spoil your looks
Ill-intentioned forward tide
Uninvited from outside
Yet another senseless war
Seen so many times before.

In Memory of Richard Dadd

Poor Dadd
He went mad
So sad
But I bet
He was set
Some way free
Of you and me
An escape
All agape
To paint flowers
In the hours
And the folk
In the smoke.

The Lifeboat House Art Gallery
for Nicholas Charles Williams

Inside the darkened studio space
There rules a strong and driven ace
Brain part-stilled by multi-sound
So that the rest may be unbound
So that his painting can go free
Hard to understand, maybe.

Outside the seabirds wheel and shriek
Wind driven spindrift, hide and seek
A stretch of sea, so blue so green
A kindergarten seaside scene
A stretch of sea so green so blue
A question, who has been here, who?

The saints of the sea, the lifeboat men
For this small building sheltered then
The local lifeboat, held inside
Manned by men who lived and died
Those selfless saints, the saints of the sea
Would give their lives for he or she
Bred in the format year on year
Ignore the threat, ignore the fear.

And when that other boat goes down
My tough old father cries
He sits beside the old TV
And tears fall out of his eyes
And I the same in another place
A bond and many weep
Before we turn the last light out
And try for sorrowed sleep
Oh those brave men, the lifeboat men
That small and stricken town
Which in imagination now
In some way wears a crown.

The Cornish coast so rocked and cliffed
A Jabberwocky jungle
So ragged and jagged, a dangerous gift
Be certain not to bungle
For on those cliffs and on those rocks
If luck draws back and fortune mocks
Lost in the darkness, caught by the gale
Engine abandoned, tattered sail
Forced ashore on a thundering tide
Wilderness stretching on either side
Ships and people have died, my dear,
All through the centuries, year by year
People and ships have died.

In the lifeboat building the painter is back
No daylight allowed, it must be all black
The windows are covered, the doors are locked
Exit and entrance both equally blocked
Multiple wiring all over the floors
The music soars and ripples and roars
Acoustically untainted.
Décor is savage and blotched and strange
No time to stop and re-arrange
So the walls are long unpainted
But there is the occupant working away
A man with sloth unacquainted
A man with a rigorous purpose in life
Determined, aspiring, as keen as a knife
And he walks in the steps of the lifeboat men
Doing his damnedest as they did then.

And There's This

Some people
Hold in themselves
An ocean
Allow them this
Do not bite
They will shed
Their own true light
Clouded or clear
Around and around
Year by year
Revel, my dear.

Looking Like This

He reclines in the chair
Thick white shirt
Black jeans
Right ankle on left knee
Mind wandering?
Time squandering?
No.
Working not shirking
No layabout he.

He has crimson socks
Thick white hair
A silver buckle
And an idea
A design to work out
To think about
Yes
Working not shirking
An artist you see.

      And
Here's looking at thee.

Brain Strangle

A fine black suit he wore
And a brilliant shirt, striped
White hair
Black suit
Rampageous shirt
She, dying to flirt
Husband there, nothing dare
Possibility of furious glare
Emotions tangle
Brain strangle

Merry Widow's Song

I saw hazily
How it could have been
Had I lived my life with you
And not that other —
Lonely in the world
Disregarded to admit happiness
Sombre, always wanting,
Triumphant when having
(was it a victory, then?)
and clumsy —
what mutilation he attempted
to those he thought should love him
as they sometimes did.

Do I Love You?

a pragmatic perception
           of
a persistent pursuivant

Do I love you?
No I don't
I never shall
and I always won't.

The Figurehead

He stands in the fierce wind
White hair blowing
Secure in his remaining strength.

Below, waves crash and tumble.
Is he, perhaps, painting?
Unravelling colours, framing
The wild and formless movements
Of this racing sea?

The world vibrates in the gale
Everything shaken, wind-pressed
Not him though, not he.

For John Raynes, effortlessly projecting an aura of immense invincibility.

Reading Poetry in Middle of Night

I float in words
A hippo* in lilies
Threatened below
By pike
Encircled above
By kingfishers

Words squeak and tumble
Mice in brain
Or rumble
Double bass players
Orchestral mumble
Gain

Poem arrive
Face of friend
So glad see you
Here you are
Door ajar
Greeting send

Poem arrive
Face of foe
Tell you something
Don't want know
Need not stay
Go away

Here another
Somebody's mother
All dressed up
Extraordinary hues
Apparently fat
Unbothered by that
Multiple bracelets
Emerald shoes.

Words that flame
Like a fire in a pyre
Cancel the ominous
funeral attire
Some will glitter
Swing in air
Removal of litter
Image laid bare
Speed your way
Enjoy the glare.

I lie there
Twisted in comfort
Relaxed
Could say pole-axed
Reverberate like
A beaten drum
Shall I deny
This omnipotent hum
Allow the sated mind
To numb?

Yes I'll retire now
Beat a retreat
To the ultimate purposeful
Towers of sleep

written when face bruised black as result of fall

Poem Before Breakfast
Unasked for advice to the young — with peculiar grammar.

Well, you see what it say
Do you know what it mean?
Do it clarify your
Own particular scene?
Do it bring a reaction,
A frisson, a buzz?
For myself I should say
That it probably does
Yes myself I should say
It quite probably will
Perhaps with a hiccup
A hitch or a spill
Do it strengthen your daylight
And darken your night?
Illuminate something
With sudden insight?
Arrive with a halo
Arrive with a breeze
Well, if it do not
Achieve any of these
If it do not achieve
Any of this
Not lessen your sorrows
Nor add to your bliss
Ignore it, my dear
Don't envelop that text
Just scrap it, my dear
And get on with the next.
You cannot take everything
Sailing aboard
Be picky, be choosy
Be trim and assured
And if you do warily
seek for your pleasure
You'll find that you slowly
Accumulate treasure.

Poem during Breakfast

That particular poem with peculiar grammar
Came into my head with the force of a hammer,
A specialized tool for upholstery wrought
A delicate purpose completely unsought
From where do they come, irresistible words
That incline to arrive in the morning as birds
For a crumb, for a worm, for a reason to fly
A benevolent task when the spirits are high.
They're demanding, insistent, entangle your day
Do anything else and they get in the way.
Sit down, get a pen, there's a poem to make
And when you have done it, go back to the cake,

I can't do it now I must shop in the town
Forget that, my darling, just please write it down
Oh can't you relent, let me finish this letter
Of course not, my dear, for the poem must get better
You hapless old woman, priorities wrong
You've a poem in your head with the strength of a gong
Don't think you can stop it, suppose it will cease
If that's what you think you belong with the geese
Unnerving suspicion, oh, here comes another
Encourage it dearie, there's no need to smother
But what of the dishes, the washing, the cake?
Irrelevant when there's a poem to make.

Poem after Breakfast
The Huge Space*

Poetry's not a ruled affair
For tunnelled academics
Good heavens, no, it's winged and charged
And riots like epidemics
Its feathers fly with peacock cry
Or endless sweet amusing
The verbal roar, the twist and soar
Of it can be confusing.
But seize it as it rushes by
And hold it in your brains
It germinates inside that fort
Can shelter you from rains
Its import may be polished clear
Or sometimes quite obscure
Though balanced so convincingly
By that esteemed allure
It radiates so constantly
A lightening in the sky
And if one day you want to
You could do worse than try
You might find a poem arriving
Much arranging much contriving
It may dislocate attention for a time.
You may sometimes feel the flutter
The approaching crack and stutter
The enchanting stop and clutter of a rhyme.
No, poetry's not a ruled affair
For those with senses shut
So let it get a hold on you
And jerk you from your rut.

endless room for poems.

Blissfully O.T.T. in One's Eighties

This sort of an addiction is
No sort of an affliction but instead
Assumes a brilliant kind of right
That shines my way
Each tinselled day
Illuminates each unexpected night.
Over the top, the top of the world
As the swanky dreamboat flies.
The fever and fun of the falling in love
The green below and the blue above
Canary bird and turtle dove
The fairy lights and candles
The gold and silver sandals
And the azure blue door handles
And the scented Coromandels

Begin again on a differing chime
The truffles and the lollipops
Feather mops and spinning tops
A silent buzz that never stops
A changing quest among the shops
I hope I don't forget this space
So far removed from the usual pace
Flowers appearing twice as bright
Though seen in exactly the same daylight
Never any thought of winning
Never any need for sinning
I did not think this would happen to me
But you do somehow set me free
Thank you dearest, thank you life

And thank God you don't
Want a wife.

Over the Top Again

Now I want nothing from you
That you don't wish to give
Just to know you're there
Is quite enough for me to live
In happy expectation
That perhaps I'll see you soon
And in the meantime, well my dear
It's Moon and June and swoon

For you are with me all the time
If only in my head
I remember how you look
And I remember what you said
That particular condition
Is itself a sort of bliss
Because it's such a luxury
To have someone to miss.

I wish you to have everything
That you could want or need
Lots of music, lots of books
Whole libraries to read
Silk shirts and ties and all that stuff
In quite excessive numbers
And handsome silk pyjamas
To ornament your slumbers

Of course a very splendid car
Perhaps a large Mercedes
So you can drive about in it
With children and old ladies
Now all you've got to do, my dear
Is be, my dear, just be
Is this condition going to last?
Well, we'll just have to see

We haven't got much future
Not a lot of time to come
For you are seventy-nine my dear
And I am eighty- one
But every time you come to call
I fall into a quake
There's nothing in my head except
Oh Lord! For heaven's sake

Perhaps

Kissing you
Was something else again
So unexpected
You did not kiss me when you came
And if you had it would not perhaps
Have been the same
But when you left
You put your arms around me
And kissed me on both cheeks and I felt
Well —
I felt rested.

If I could hold you
And you could hold me
For half an hour perhaps
At least that
We could have some music perhaps
And dance a little
Although you might step on my toes
Or I on yours
For we have never danced
Although we both love dancing
But if I could hold you
For twenty minutes even
I should not feel perhaps
in this twenty-first century
So over-tested.

The unreliable technology
If not already broken
Breaks
The uncertain world quakes
Repairs are a gamble involving a preamble
A deadly ramble
Round half-understood probabilities
Or improbabilities perhaps
Advice often rot

Try it or not?
A hideous gavotte
Phone rings nobody there
Answer not requested

Trusted establishments go astray
In a way they never did
Until today
Banks, for instance, making errors
Pestered by computer terrors
Phone rings nobody there
Airwaves infested.

Go to hospital, get ill
Here my dear another pill
Savage bugs, conflicting drugs
Doctors struggle, quicksand generalisations
Holidays a great relief
Renovate their self-belief
Often suggested.

And the unfortunate children
Monsters instead of fairies
Surely a poor exchange
"I'll buy myself a gun,"
the ten year old thought
counting up his money
as he had been taught
"Shoot someone, that'll be fun
a thing to be done
why not?"
Violence ingested.

But when you kissed me
I saw a garden, just a glimpse
A November garden perhaps
Everything rather brown
It was not my garden
It belonged to you and she

Whom you married all those years ago
With whom you had children
All those years ago
Who loves and looks after you
Now
Her life invested.

No it is not my garden
I would never have a garden like that
But it seems I can catch a glimpse
Through the gate
When you kiss me.

N.B

It could be a gate into a prison perhaps
That garden had high walls
But if I could hold you
For even a few minutes perhaps
And you could hold me
Attention arrested
Would I know?
Would I want to?
Perhaps.

What Has Happened?

What has happened, what's going on?
Population put upon
Is it all those damn computers
wretched common sense polluters?
Hardly know where to start
where to throw an opening dart
direct the angled inquisitions —
let's begin with the opticians.

Could see with old glasses
now insufficiently strong
can't see with new glasses
everything blurred, all wrong
told, question of distance
put up stubborn resistance
they withdrew, conferred, referred
our glasses right, they averred
returning
your eyes wrong
What? What?
And there was more
a frightful bore
explanations offered, diagnosis proffered.
No one concurred, emotions stirred
could not understand a word
ongoing confusions, no conclusions.
decisions protested.
Tried other place, glasses better
made by young well-dressed go-getter
gratitude manifested
case rested.

And what has happened to eating apples
what has happened to them?
Picked too soon? Kept too cold?

lost their taste
flavour old
enjoyment molested.

And all these catalogues
several a day, that's silly
must accept them willy-nilly
throw them away.
What has happened to lavatory seats?
used to last for ages
now they slip askew
loose screw
inciting domestic rages
serenity bested.

Girls get drunk, self-respect sunk
or changed, re-arranged
ugly music, ungainly dancing
strained distorted prancing
passing fad?
Hope so,
not interested.

Dustbin numbers replicate
organized to complicate
parking problems throng and thrive
imprison you inside your drive
much detested.

What next, what more
what added trials
extra printed miles
new fangled renditions
barnacled
with new conditions
relentless perditions?
Prognosis requested.

The Handsome Irish Gardener

The garden came out in a thousand visions
All except one naked wall
Despoiled by an Irish gardener
Who stripped off its coverings all
And there it stood, bereft, bereaved
Blocks of cement, untwigged, unleaved
Unattractive appearance, a shocking glare
To my outraged and furious eye laid bare
I fiercely complained with distress and derisions
I railed against his excessive excisions.
"Had to, ma'am." he decisively said
A grimace on his face and a shake of his head
As he stood in the flower bed, foot on a plant
He may forgive himself, I just can't.

Then he suddenly asked with a hint of a smile
"Will I take you out dancing, ma'am, once in a while?"
A beautiful Irishman, son of the earth
And I rather old but a daughter of mirth
And the dance such a permanent passion of mine
For a heartbeat of life is the dancing line
The sounds of the vineyard, the scents of the sea
Past memories of pastimes came rushing past me
But there, of course was the naked wall
No interconnecting the two at all.

I wrestled with these conflicting divisions
Unable to deal with such sudden decisions
"How kind," I said calmly though still in a rage
But I felt a slight flutter, emotions engage
A sort of acceptance, be careful I beg
But the tilt of his chin and the turn of his leg
I looked at him standing there, sweater and jeans
Imagined a few unacceptable scenes
Beginning to wonder just where might this lead
This dancing and everything, better take heed.
He was looking at me with a light in his eye
He suspected, I thought, I was tempted to try

A shift of the shoulder, the hint of a bow
Be careful old woman, that then this is now
For as I was eighty and really quite weighty
I'd peacefully thought I was running to seed
I'd been writing and reading and pruning and weeding
For dancing and loving I'd not felt a need
And I didn't anticipate more of that stuff
For my life had contained what I thought was enough.

I thought of the wall and I thought of the plant
I thought of it all and I worried
For I didn't want to do anything rash
Nor be made to do anything hurried
If I asked him to lunch and he offered a bunch
I had quite a strong hunch if it came to the crunch
If we drank some wine and were feeling fine
My emotions might lurch, our fingers entwine
And I'd fall off my perch and get flurried.

Well.....

What with this and the other I fell in a panic
And what I'd been thinking seemed downright Satanic
It was quite a long time since, emotions uncurled
I had passed a few hours with my feathers unfurled
And I, merry widow, quite happy and free
And he, a bit younger, as strong as a tree —
I thought, "Oh dear, but I might fall to pieces
Leave all that to great-nephews and nieces.

I thought of the plant and I thought of the wall
And I thought of the dancing, thought of it all
Perhaps he would and perhaps he wouldn't
But I became fairly sure that I shouldn't
I finally thought that I wouldn't at all
And before that depressing defoliate wall
I finally found that I couldn't.

The Heart
reflections on the relatively unemotional nature of....

The heart I have has never spoken
And fortunately never broken
It simply lies inside my chest
Fitting in with all the rest

It's never been inclined to melt
No fancy sentiments has felt
The dear old thing is quite prosaic
Part of the physical mosaic

To say a heart is cold or hot
Is simply to be talking rot
It does not ever rise or sink
Is not, of course, designed to think

It will at times go pit-a-pat
And never seems the worse for that
But finer feelings, no no no,
It just keeps beating, fast or slow.

Well, that is no surprise to you
For that is all it's meant to do
And if sometimes it seems to ache
I ate too much, for heaven's sake.

So if he tells thee, hand on heart
That thou the Queen of Beauty art
It really should not cause a ripple
The hand is merely on a nipple.

And if I wish you all the best
Send lots of love with honest zest
It's not my heart that got it said
But what goes on inside my head.

Sad Song - Glad Song
for Anne Curtis

My knee's all swollen
Oh dear
But it doesn't hurt much
They've given me painkillers
Don't need a crutch
Find an elegant stick
Get used to it quick.

Can't scrub kitchen floor
Oh dear
Been doing it for years
No more
Flip flop, slip slop
Good habit to drop
Change to mop
Don't know why
I didn't before

Can't dig garden
Oh dear
But shan't really rue it
Determination harden —
Find someone else to do it
After all, I'm more
Than half-way through it
My life I mean
I'll do some of the rest
Pots for instance
Some more pots
Always liked that best
Must take care now
Not to be tied up in knots

Mustn't forget it
Or upset it
The knee, I mean
Must aid and abet it
Look after me
As well as the others
Novel thought
Last on list of many mothers
Never felt I ought
Opportunity now, unsought
No digging, no scrubbing
Life less fraught
Except for knee, of course
And anyway
Gave up all those games
The rushing and smashing
The twisting and crashing
Years ago
Now have different aims
A studio.

The Luncheon Guest
for Vivian Prideaux

Vivian came to lunch today
She wore a gorgeous dress
The sort of dress that makes a day
Supremely more than less
Made of a magic black stuff
Stiff to hold the shape
Traffic stop - but not the sort
To cause unkindly gape
Down each side from hip to hem
Were insets gently swishing
To covet is a sin, we know
But no escape from wishing

One side pleated scarlet silk
And opposite was russet
Design so elegant and plain
Additions did not fuss it
And these insertions, subtly stitched
So they were mostly hidden
The effect, in essence rather bold
Did not escape unbidden
A twist of talent made quite sure
That all was well-controlled.
A sudden movement, step or turn
Exciting pleated flare
A minimal hint of see-through
To add a dash of dare

Lovely lady, come again
And ornament the day
Such welcome visions add to life's
Unquenchable array.

Henman on court

He plays his own unusual game
Nobody else's quite the same
He plays like a solicitor's son
Gauging the aspects one by one
He plays with a cleverness hard to achieve
Contrived with a subtlety hard to believe
Experienced with downs and ups
Tournaments, titles, Davis Cups
Matchless matches, thrilling patches
Advance and retreat in worrying snatches
Fabulous Tim, a hero heady
Brilliant game at times unsteady
Fans aligned on Henman Hill
Poised to celebrate his skill
The Centre Court, his own domain
Triumph, agitation, pain
Spectators gathered, schooled for strain
Appreciate the tennis brain
Appreciate the agile feet
Nimble, practised, neat and fleet
The courage, the essential guts
The ifs and buts, the clips and cuts
The effort and determination
To reach eventual destination

Knock-up ended, match begins
(Oh I do hope Henman wins)
Fine opponent, instinct blazing
Commendable athletic phrasing
Inclinations soon discovered
Possible weaknesses uncovered
Tactical network swiftly spreading
Through the mazes swiftly threading
He'll hit it there you think
Quite wrong
He'll hit it elsewhere
Slightly long

Should have gone right but no it didn't
Should have been good but no it wasn't
That was a shot, oh that was ripping
Back to baseline skipping, skipping
Fearsome drive and angle angle
Get opponent in a tangle
Forty thirty now, break point
Miss return and disappoint
Opponent runs and leaps and races
Aim to put him through his paces
Using unexpected spaces
Tie him up in mental knot
Overhead and passing shot
Close the set as like as not,
Such excitement, tension mounting
Oh for that shot no accounting
This one flattened out too much
Temporary lack of touch
He's lost the game, he's lost the set
News we hear with trained regret
Still, no need to be downhearted
Match has really hardly started.

Now we're in the second set
Adversary serves a let
Then a fault and he's in trouble
Next one's out, he's served a double
Solo voices, "Go on, Tim"
"Go on Tim" encourage him
Thankfully the weather's good
Brilliant sunshine, knock on wood
Adversary tripped and fell
Hitting grass with stifled yell
Backhand's going rather wide
Try one on the other side
Opponent's errors, Henman's guide
That was a resplendent serve
Ending with elaborate swerve
Hits a lob a bit too low

Just within the reach of foe
Understandable frustration
Try to keep your concentration
Try again to be consistent
Calm, industrious, persistent
On occasion go for broke
Annihilate the other bloke
Crafty hint of mouse and cat
Just over net an elegant tap
That one hard to put away
Dropping ball, so tough to play
Results in total disarray.
Games with service, arduous haul
Time for tie-break, six games all
Children watch, attention rapt
Seniors, strength as yet unsapped
Next in line a sleeping mother
Don't wake up he's lost another.

Two sets down and he's a menace
Memorable sight in tennis
This way that way, balls are speeding
Senses sharpened, stress unheeding
Serve and volley - serve - stay back
Down the sideline, special knack
Hm, that point to be contested
Doubtful call of course detested
Hawk-eye proving quite a blessing
Wonderful for rage-repressing
These forgivable distractions
Should not prejudice reactions
Any possible infractions
Followed by confirmed retractions
Hits a winner, seldom sounder
Adversary flip and flounder
Ha! a really splendid get
Graceful skim across the net

Now a dashing cross court volley
Lost the point, a touch of folly
Heavens, an eccentric bounce
Opportunity to pounce
Now he rushes to the net
To smash the ball at speed of jet
Dear oh dear that shot was out
Sharp return and turnabout
Henman Henman clap clap clap
Sent that blinder through a gap
Hope not make another error
Crowd immobilized with terror
Henman Henman clap clap clap
Wakes that mother from her nap
Every one in frightful flap
But there's no need to fuss and fret
Because at last he's won a set

Swish and slither, dip and dash
Tries to get it, has a bash
Good return, extremely quick
Lands with unexpected kick
Everybody finds it trying
Living and dying
Sobbing and crying
Mopping eyes and wringing hands
Consternation in the stands
Clutching friend, no longer looking
Tell me, tell me what is cooking?
Now a love game, serving massive
Famous face remains impassive
Ace right down the centre line
No emotion, not a sign
Angles flashing to and fro
Where to next, one cannot know
Adversary broken reed

Unforced errors, lost the lead
Now he's got to find a way
To bring his forehand into play
Henman plays with tireless flair
A kind of calculated dare
No need now to fret and dither
All is well, he's won another.

Here it is, the final set
Of this furious duet
Henman, Henman clap clap clap
All his brilliant shots on tap
Genius genius quite unique
Sort of tennis hide and seek
Too much lift, sudden wind drift
All askew and slightly miffed
Hesitation, moan from crowd
Mostly muffled, not too loud
Go on Tim you've nearly done it
Oh my God he's nearly won it
Go on Tim, go on Tim
Match in balance, on the rim
Lost match point, hope dissipated
Lost another, so frustrated
All his fans, poised to salute
Thousands shattered, heart in boot
Now attention final shot
Opponent tries but hits it not
He's won, he's won, delirious fun
Unbelievers on the run
What a blessing, what relief
So much bliss beyond belief
Now we hear that frantic roar
No one could imagine more
Everyone beside themselves
Heaven is here
Stand up and cheer.

So thank you, dear Tim Henman
Providential starry Brit
You've given us mass enjoyment
You've really done us proud
You'll never be forgotten
For we'll remember well
That on Wimbledon and country
You have cast repeated spell
We knew when first we saw you
That our lives would be improved
So please don't leave these islands
For we don't want you removed
We hope that you will flourish
Have many final flings
And countless halcyon moments
On the roundabouts and swings
We hope to hear much more of you
And lovely-looking wife
Enjoy what you get up to
For remainder of your life.

The Seagull Scene
for Judith Morris

The further away they are
the more beautiful they become
flying so high, so far
sweeping around the sky
with wild authoritative cry
early morning fly-past
eye-level, arrow-fast
off on air patrol
or variously perching
young ones not yet airborne
insecurely lurching
roof-top, flip flop
roof-skating, dangerous
fumble, tumble — fall
to the careless world below.

The mammas and the papas
are occasionally ferocious
turbulent and fierce
unbecomingly atrocious
cold, unfeeling, wheeler-dealing
wing-swing, chimney stack
landscape look-outs, sentinels
violent shriek, sudden screech
strident scream seagull speech
domestic chatter, cackle, babble
raucous squawk, seagull talk
a capacious language
swans of the air?
Perhaps not
but passing fair.

An Arboreal Triumph

That little palm tree
about four feet high
lives on their small flat roof
God knows why
unless it's to please my eye
up there, anything but weatherproof
they won't see it very well
how it's doing they can't tell
it's outside their bathroom window
decent, heavy patterned glass
bit of a horticultural farce.

That little tree
in a pot beside the sea
and to its rooftop pinned
withstanding climatic terrorism
immoderate high wind
horizontal rain blast
wild salt-burdened gale
freezing from Russia
flying air, shriek and wail
is an example of heroism.

Heaven knows the poor little thing
looks likely to take wing
crash on the concrete
subject to violent mangles
blown from all compass angles
this way that day
that way this day
having no voice
has no choice
must remain in its awkward position
its unheeded symbolic condition
nobody to see
except me
powerfully affected —

so much all over the place
is unprotected
yet we must not forget
more protection less freedom

Taking a Walk

Old Doris went out yesterday
First time for ages
Been ill you see
Shaky old lady, quaky old lady
Set off, nervous
If they were to see me
I know what they would say
Rash improper dangerous prank
Misbehaving old crank
Carers, minders, friends and so on
Much experience to go on
All been only kind

But off she went just the same
Weather heaven-sent
Stubborn old dame
Couldn't go fast even with stick
How long last?
Tired so quick
Garden gate, hurdle passed
Push it open, shut it fast
Caution out and overcast
A little aghast
See some bluebells, see the stream
Water running water gleam
Sunshine glitter, grasses glimmer
Single fallen feather shimmer
Birds drifting, earth shifting
Wavery old lady, quavery old lady
Flowers wafting, yellow white
Well-rembered sight
Down the lane, legs complain
Now she must go back again
Wobbly old lady, knobbly old lady
An angular soul
Heading for goal
Garden gate, hurdle passed
Push it open, shut it fast

Tomorrow
If stronger
Go for longer.

A Strange Remark (geriatric hoo ha)

As I was going to the supermarket
to buy strawberries
no cream
I have them with top milk these days
It's one of my slimming little ways
I came face to face with an old man
in the crowd
old and bowed
"I'll rice you to the fence." he croaked
staring at me
This didn't make sense
there wasn't a fence
there wasn't any rice either
that I could see.
"What?" I said
he repeated his remark, quite loud
staring at me
I shook my head
"What do you think I said?" he enquired
Curiosity fired
I repeated his remark, quite loud
We were both a bit deaf, I and he
At least I supposed we might be
Well, I knew I was, a bit.
"Oh," he said nodding, "No.
I'll RACE you to the fence"
I was enlightened
Expression brightened
There still wasn't a fence
But clarity, hilarity
"Well, I've got one thing to say to you." I joked
"What's that?"
"I bet you'd win."
Said with the hint of a grin
He looked at me with gratitude
Had he feared I might be rude?
"Oh well, my 'at." he said
"I dunno 'bout that."
Mumbling and muttering
"I dunno about that." he said
and the crowd moved on.

Medical Students

Three arrive
Good-looking lads
Quite nice clothes, nothing she loathes
Very polite.
"Good morning." "Morning." "How are you?
Hope you had a decent night?"
"Thank you, thank you, kind to ask."
Face an inexpressive mask
What do these three
want with me?
"We've come to take a blood sample."
Do they, then, require an armful?
"What, all of you?" an arm extended
"Feel free, I'll try not to screech."
Humour, however, out of reach
No reaction, quite impassive
Inexperience clearly massive
"Try not cause you any pain."
Fumble with arm
"Oh dear, can't seem to find a vein."
"Surely there must be one there?"
Sympathetic stare.
"Yes but - well, you have a try
Hands along to number two
"Perhaps have better luck with you."
"Well I wonder, is this it?"
Tiniest of needle prick
Tries once more, minimal gore
"Not entirely sure."
"Afraid I bruise quite easily."
She mentions
Polarizing their attentions
"Apparently to do with pills
symptoms of my current ills."
They peer at arm uneasily
"Here's a tissue, use to blot."
Got it right as like as not

"How are you feeling?
Are you all right?
Need a rest?
Would that be best?
Or shall we try the other arm
Don't think we're doing any harm."
"Oh I'm sure not, carry on please."
Tries other side, a hopeful squeeze
Unexpected indecision
Much elusive imprecision

Finally they go away
Try again another day
"Goodbye, goodbye, get well quick."
"Thank you so much." (rather thick?)
Next day, looking, what see there?
Sort of map, Australia fair
Other arm, same blackish hue
India, Africa, large in view
"Look at this." she says to nurse
"Am I heading for a hearse?
Only bruises, doesn't hurt."
Starchy lady, slightly curt
Stifled sniff, "They're only young
Feet upon a lowly rung
Got to start, it's only fair
Everybody start somewhere."
"Well," she says, "It's plain to see
Yesterday the start was me."

Being Ill

When I'm ill
I seem to lose myself.
What's left
is a remnant in a hole
a black hole
like the well in the yard
of our house in Ireland
which only had water
when it rained

Discovery

I really thought
that when I was eighty
I'd have calmed down a bit
oh yes.... but no
not a bit of it
here I am, here I sit
and dance if I have the chance
brain battered
but functioning still
emotions boom and zoom
inhabit expanding room
crescendo, innuendo
go where they will
up and down the hill
take me along for the ride
different slant, different slide
universal aunt
substitute mother
and some of the other
oh yes.... oh no
the winds do blow
still.

The Bus Load

They disengage themselves
with, it must be said,
understandable fuss
from the bus.
But what has befallen them
have they been rolled in dust
beige and grey become a must?
There's a sprinkle of toad green
to expand the faded scene.
Do they say, when faced with colour
I'll have that one, please, it's duller?
They issue forth, a muddy stream
lacking flourish, lacking gleam.
It's a group of O.A.P.s
Mustn't censure, mustn't tease
But where's the blue
the mellow yellow?
Crimson costs no more than drab
Where the thousand shades and shadows
of a multi-million flowers
which could brighten up these saddoes
these enduring sweets and sours?
There's no need to be garish
You do not want to glare
Of course
not walk along the pavement
and collect a curious stare
But dear old senior ladies
why this need for cheerless tat?
Please, a little touch of lipstick
and perhaps a foreign hat
For heaven's sake, whatever else
keep off the tramline hair
and don't forget
not yet, not yet
you are the clothes you wear

And men, restrain those razors
grey beards, discreetly shaped
are often most attractive
a telling bit of dash
and perhaps a foreign hat?

Oh please do
stop depressing us and you.

Why Both?

I play Bach, I play Boogie
Any similarities
Between these disparities
One so arranged
And from the other so estranged?
Not a lot
You can listen to them, dance perhaps
Banish the silence
What about words, for instance
Words for Bach
Music sprung from convention
Illuminated by invention
Bursting from bounds, from bonds
Waterfalls, wing-footed torrents
Momentous breakneck currents
Sometimes a tranquil and luxuriant lake
Closely ordered
Even small ponds
Inspirational sound, absolutely
A roar in the brain
Heaven just above
Such an intellect
So academically grand
So intricately correct
So hard to play with clarity
Sufficient intention and respect
On occasion, simple
A slight rain
A tinkling trifle
For dancing, in a minor key
Perfection always

And what about the boogie, then
What words for that?
It's a roar in the head all right
An uproar, you could say
Hear it, have a drink
Dance through the night
Sprung from African races
Shovelled as slaves to America's cotton
Living in format of inherited disgraces
From which they have emerged
From whence this music surged
Harmonically uncluttered - polyrhythmic
Strong, exuberant, direct
Instinctive energy unchecked
Strike up in crowded room
See them jerk, assemble themselves
What's this?
Riotous, revel-rousing, frantic, sparky
Improvisational, sensational, larky
Of course must have both
A question of extremes
An enrichment of dreams
A swing to and fro, let go, let go
A musical skateboard half-pipe
Change as good as a holiday?
That's it.
Enjoy.

The Dream

I dreamed one night
I was walking through an underpass
somewhat dank and dreary
as these places are
I was weary
but could see light
and came out onto a path
sloping upwards
banks on either side, some flowers,
to a gate at the top
a garden gate, bending trees
and an old man standing there
white hair
I toiled on up
"Come along now, my dear,"
he said, arm extended
"I have been waiting a long time
for you."
I took his hand, I kissed his cheek
it was my grandfather
who died when I was three
he had indeed been waiting long
eighty years since last we met.
It seems that infant love does not forget
It's there for life
and longer?

Jenefer taken 30 years ago...

...of course, she hasn't changed a bit

Jenefer Ann Murray spent many years within the stitched textile community, had work selected for international exhibitions in France, Hungary, Germany, Canada and has shown in various places all over England.

Jenefer is also an LRAM, veering wildly between J.S. Bach and boogie-woogie, and a Cordon Bleu cook. However, pasties have been her favourite food since shortly after she was born.